Everything You Need to Know About

DECISION-MAKING

Although you make decisions every day, some, such as whether or not to take the cigarette your best friend offers you, are more difficult than others.

Everything You Need to Know About

DECISION-MAKING

Julie Parker

THE ROSEN PUBLISHING GROUP, INC.
NEW YORK

Published in 1996 by The Rosen Publishing Group, Inc.
29 East 21st Street, New York, NY 10010

First Edition

Manufactured in the United States of America

Library of Congress Cataloging-in-Publication Data

Parker, Julie F.
    Everything you need to know about decision making / Julie Parker.
—1st ed.
      p. cm. — (The need to know library)
    Includes bibliographical references and index.
    Summary: Briefly discusses the process of decision-making,
emphasizing real situations in which teenagers may find themselves.
    ISBN 0-8239-2055-0
    1. Decision-making in adolescence—Juvenile literature.
[1. Decision-making.] I. Title. II. Series.
BF724.3.D47P37   1995
153.8′13—dc20   95-14904
                                  CIP
                                   AC

Contents

Making your own decisions, such as how much money you can afford to withdraw and spend, is a large part of becoming an adult.

Chapter 1

Making Decisions and Growing Up

A lot of growing up is about making your own decisions. When you were very young, someone (probably your parent[s]) decided everything for you. The chances are that you had little say about whom you saw, what you wore, or where you went. But now that you are older, you determine what you do most of the time. And in addition to figuring out your daily routine, you are beginning to look to the future.

You may have heard adults say things like, "You kids have it easy," or "Enjoy your life while you're this age," or "Youth is wasted on the young." Some grown-ups tend to romanticize the teenage years as full of fun and friends, and free from problems and responsibilities. The truth is, however, that you are making some important decisions now that will affect the rest of your life. You may be debating what to do after graduation or even

whether you should finish high school. You might
be thinking about getting a job or choosing a
college. Maybe you are wondering about when to
have sex, or perhaps get married. You may be
trying to figure out what you want to be doing in
five or ten years. If you think about all these big
decisions at once, it can feel overwhelming.

But making decisions doesn't have to be scary.
Choosing the right option is a skill that can be
learned and practiced. Much like playing a musical
instrument, the more you work at making good
decisions the better you will be at it. This book is
designed to help you develop the habit of choosing
what is right for you.

Big and Little Decisions

Deciding to read this book probably did not feel
like a big deal. Often you make small decisions,
like what to read, without giving them much
thought. However, small decisions are valuable
because they help you get in the practice of
making good choices. Without even realizing it,
you are probably used to making choices that help
or hurt you.

Many serious problems, such as taking drugs or
breaking the law, can be traced to the pattern of
someone's making bad decisions for herself or
himself. On the other hand, successful people are
those who choose well for themselves and plan

Small decisions, such as what book to read, help prepare you for the big decisions you'll have to make in life, such as what career to choose.

their future. Even when decisions are small, they are part of a larger picture.

Big decisions are more obvious and usually require a lot of thought. Deciding about having sex, working full time, getting married, buying a car, going to college, or whether or not to have a baby are just some examples. You may spend hours, days, or weeks wondering what to do. You may seek advice from other people or stay awake at night, unsure of what is right. Some people have a hard time making up their minds about big decisions because they get caught up trying to please everyone. Often they forget about themselves—the person who is most affected. Big decisions are those that have a lasting result in *your* life.

Developing This Skill

Life is full of both big and little decisions. As you face them, it helps to have a process. A series of steps for making decisions is explained fully in Chapter 5. It involves figuring out what you want, exploring your options, gathering information, writing down your reasons, and taking the time you need. You might ask other people for their opinions, but you need to know how to tell the difference between good input and bad advice. At the same time, remember that you are the expert on what is best for you. Also you are the one who

You can ask other people for their opinions on a decision you must make, but the final choice is up to you.

gains or loses as a result of what you decide. When you have a process that takes all this into account and you learn how to use it well, you will be equipped with a valuable lifetime skill.

Allowing others to make decisions for you is called being passive.

Chapter 2

Taking Responsibility

If making decisions is so great, then how come so many people don't want to do it? Sometimes people are so afraid of making a mistake that they don't take responsibility for their decisions. Instead of thinking about a situation, they let their action (or lack of action) determine the outcome. Some of these habits of behavior can hurt themselves or others. Because of this, it can be good to recognize these patterns and see if you use them yourself.

Being Passive

How often have you heard someone ask, "What do you want?" and the other person says, "I don't care," or "I'm easy," or "Whatever"? The person who is not expressing his or her opinion is being *passive*. He or she does not want to make a

13

decision and so pretends that it doesn't matter. This may seem like the easy way out, but really it is just the opposite.

Destin is unsure if he should continue with Spanish in his senior year. He likes the class and is doing well, but he will already have enough credits to graduate without this extra course. One day in the cafeteria Destin and his friend Steve are discussing their schedules.

"You know, I'm wondering if I should stick with Spanish next year . . ." Destin begins.

"¿Por qué, man?" Steve asks. "We're going to be seniors, *which means we're supposed to have fun, remember? Why make life harder on yourself? Give yourself a break—you deserve it. Relax a little."*

"I guess you're right," Destin mutters. "I'll just take it easy and drop the class."

Destin's big mistake here is being passive, which is unfair to everyone involved. He cheats himself because he learns less and misses out on a class he enjoys. Later on if Destin ends up regretting his decision, he may blame Steve, which would also be unfair.

While this example tells of just one small incident, many people are in the habit of being passive throughout their lives. Their decisions are made by whatever another person or group suggests. They might do this out of an overeagerness to please someone else, even at their own expense. Perhaps they are so used to letting others decide that they don't take time to stop and consider, "Hey, what do *I* want here?" When it is time to make a decision, the passive person needs to stop and think seriously about what would be best for himself or herself, and then speak up.

Being Aggressive

The opposite of being passive is being *aggressive*. Aggressive people know what they want and go after it, but they think about themselves too much. They accomplish their goals at the expense of other people.

John is determined to make the honor roll in high school, just like his older sister. During the first few days of the school year, he pays careful attention to the other students in his classes to see who are the smartest. Then after each class he picks his target students and tells them that he'll be sitting near them during tests. He makes it clear that if they don't let him cheat or if they tell anyone about this threat, he'll beat them up after school.

Being aggressive, like being passive, is also unfair to everyone involved. John is mean and underhanded with the people he bullies. And he is betraying himself. By relying on someone else for the answers, he is getting less education. If the time comes when there is no one else to give the answers, or if John is caught cheating, he will have more troubles. John's unfair aggressive behavior victimizes others and robs himself.

Being Passive-Aggressive

Passive-aggressive behavior is when you say one thing, but really mean another. A passive-aggressive person pretends that whatever is decided doesn't matter to her or him *(passive)*, while single-mindedly going after something *(aggressive)*. Passive-aggressive people are dishonest with themselves and manipulate others.

Tiffany is leaving school late one afternoon, after a student government meeting. It's getting dark, and she's just thinking about that two-mile walk home, when Jeff, who is also in the student government, bounds by her jingling his car keys.

"Hey Jeff, are you going home?" Tiffany calls to him.

"Sure. What's it look like?" Jeff answers.

"Well . . . um . . . where do you live?"

"Up near the elementary school . . . why?" Jeff asks.

"Oh, I'm way across town . . . I don't want to trouble you . . . I'll just walk the two miles myself . . .

Physically aggressive behavior is easier to spot than verbal or emotionally aggressive behavior.

it probably won't be totally *dark by the time I get home . . . chances are I'll be fine . . . hopefully,"* *Tiffany says wistfully.*

Tiffany obviously wants a ride home but chooses not to come right out and ask for it. Her behavior is passive-aggressive, because she wants something and is going after it—while saying that it doesn't matter. She tries to make Jeff feel guilty for not driving her home without ever asking him if he would. Tiffany would make things a lot easier if she just decided to be forthright about what she wanted.

Being Assertive

Assertive people go after their objectives in a way that respects others and themselves. When you act assertively you state what you want honestly, while considering the feelings of others. You use "I" statements, describing your own thoughts and emotions, instead of blaming or second-guessing the other person.

Meredith's older sister, Amanda, has an eating disorder. Even though she is 5'4" and weighs 115 pounds, Amanda is convinced that she's fat. Recently Meredith has noticed Amanda going to the bathroom after dinner and locking the door for a long time. Meredith hears vomiting noises and knows that this eating disorder (bulimia) is serious and can be deadly. She wants her sister to stop, but doesn't know what to say to her.

***Passive approach**—Meredith worries about this but doesn't say anything.*

***Aggressive approach**—Meredith: "Amanda, I know that you are vomiting your dinner every night. I'm going to tell Mom and Dad and make them cut off your allowance until you stop it. I'll also go to the guidance couselor and she'll force you to get therapy or be suspended."*

***Passive-Aggressive**—"Amanda, I know you're ruining your life, but who cares? You want to starve to death—fine by me. Keep this up and before long you'll be like a skeleton. You want to look like that— swell—suit youself."*

***Assertive**—"Amanda, may I talk with you? I've heard you vomiting every night, and I'm really worried about you. I'm afraid that you are hurting yourself. Have you thought about getting some help? I care about you, and I'll do whatever I can to help."*

When you are assertive, you take responsibility for yourself and your own feelings. You know what you want to accomplish and then go for it in a way that respects others and yourself. Thinking and acting assertively are necessary for making and carrying out healthy decisions.

Chapter 3

Listening to Others

As you take responsibility for yourself, you learn how to consult with other people before making your own decision. When you need to decide something, do you ask other people for advice? Whether it's choosing an outfit for a party or a career for a lifetime, getting feedback from someone else can help you to make up your mind. Also hearing someone else's thoughts often puts things in perspective.

Good and Bad Advice

Since asking for advice is common, it is important to be able to tell the difference between good input and bad advice. Sometimes, even without realizing it, a friend may say something that is not in your best interest. You need to be able to decide what advice is helpful and what is best to ignore.

Jill and Mitchell have been going out for nine months. Now that it is summer, Mitchell's parents go away on the weekends; Mitchell has to stay home for his lifeguard job. He thinks that this would be the perfect time for him and Jill to have sex. He tells her that he loves her and that is all that matters. Jill likes Mitchell a lot—maybe she even loves him—but she is very confused about having sex. One Friday, she invites her two best friends, Veronica and Maureen, to sleep over. Late at night, when she's sure her parents are asleep, Jill asks them for their advice.

"Hey, you guys—promise you can keep a secret?" Jill begins.

"Yeah, sure, of course," Maureen and Veronica both answer. They know something juicy is coming up.

"Well . . . Mitchell wants to sleep with me . . . and I'm not sure what I should do."

"That's a secret?" asks Veronica. "Maybe to some people in Australia, but to those of us who know you it's pretty obvious what Mitchell wants. I think you should be fair to him—I mean, you've been going out for practically a year. Anyway, what's the big deal? Everyone's having sex."

"Not everyone," Maureen interrupts.

"Listen," continues Veronica, "do you want to be a virgin when you go off to college? Please. Now, as the expert here, let me tell you: Sex is not all it's cracked up to be, but I'm glad I've gotten it over with."

There are two kinds of advice: good advice and bad advice.
Determine which you are being given before making a
decision based on that advice.

*Jill thinks for a second. "Perhaps I should just get
it out of the way. I mean, Mitchell's a good guy, and
sex has become this big thing between us. It probably
wouldn't be so bad."*

*"Now wait a minute," says Maureen. "How do you
feel about having sex with him?"*

*"Well . . . the idea is not unappealing . . ." Jill
answers.*

*"If you said that about a restaurant we wouldn't
go, and I think this is a little more important,"
Maureen observes. "Besides, have you thought about
all the possible results of sex: sexually transmitted
diseases, even AIDS, or a Jill-Mitchell kiddie?"*

"How dramatic," says Veronica flatly.

"Hey, it could happen. Mitchell may not be a virgin—what about his sexual past? And no birth control is 100 percent foolproof—except for not having sex," Maureen counters. "Why don't you just wait until you know it's right for you, Jill? There's no rush."

"Maybe you're right," Jill answers. She seems relieved.

Both friends have advice for Jill—but which can help her and which might harm her? These checklists can help you tell the difference between good and bad advice.

Good Advice

- does not try to control
- causes you to think for yourself
- may steer you away from harmful options
- may provide additional information
- leaves you feeling at ease and resolved with your decision.

Bad Advice

- tries to dominate (control)
- may serve the other person's self-interest
- may lead you to harmful situations

- may withhold information
- leaves you feeling unsure and conflicted about the decision you've made
- causes you to rationalize and look for reasons why this decision would be okay.

Which friend is thinking more of Jill here—and which one is thinking of herself? Veronica tries to make up Jill's mind for her, saying that she owes sex to Mitchell. Since Veronica has already had sex and obviously doesn't feel that great about her experience, maybe she wants Jill to understand what she's been through. Veronica also doesn't tell Jill that she's sorry she had sex. Veronica had heard that sex is supposed to be wonderful, and when she remembers losing her virginity she just feels miserable. She does not think about the risks you run when you have sex, nor does she suggest that Jill think about them. When Jill first agrees to sleep with Mitchell, she makes up reasons for telling herself that this is right. This is called *rationalizing* and is a warning sign that the decision may be wrong. Also Veronica's line that "Everybody's doing it" simply is not true. Whatever "it" may be, there are always some people who think for themselves.

That is what Maureen helps Jill to do. Maureen asks Jill how she feels and points out that Jill should listen to her own mixed emotions. Maureen reminds Jill of some of the possible dangers of having sex. When Jill decides that she does not need to have sex to please someone else but should think of what she wants for herself first, she feels as if a weight has been taken off her shoulders. Feeling comfortable with a decision is usually a sign that it is right.

Where to Go for Advice

Even without realizing it, you are getting advice from lots of sources that tell you what you should do. Advertisers spend billions of dollars each year to influence your decisions about what you will eat, drink, wear, drive, and own. Famous models and sports figures urge you to purchase certain products. Since these companies and celebrities try to persuade you to spend money that goes to them, they are not reliable sources of influence. A good source of advice respects your ability to make your own decisions. Which of these sources may be the most helpful for you?

Peers (Friends Your Age)

The first place teenagers usually turn for advice is their friends. Because of this, it is important to choose your friends carefully. True friends will take the time to listen to you and show they care by their interest, support, and loyalty.

Sometimes your friends may want you to be like

Teenagers often try their first drink or drug with their friends as a result of negative peer pressure.

them, even if it means doing something harmful. The unspoken message that you should be like everyone else is called *peer pressure*. Although peer pressure is usually associated with doing something that hurts you, there is both good and bad peer pressure. For example, the pressure to smoke with friends would be bad peer pressure because smoking is an addictive habit that causes heart and lung diseases, as well as being expensive and smelly. On the other hand, the pressure to study and do well in school would be good peer pressure because it would create better possibilities for you after graduation and help you make the most of yourself.

Family

Whether or not you feel you can turn to a member of your family depends on your relationship with them. Does your mother or father take the time to listen to you, especially when you are upset? Do you have a brother or sister who understands you well? Maybe you have a relative with good judgment. Since your family members have known you from a very young age, they might understand what decision would be best for you.

Teachers and Guidance Counselors

Are there adults at your school who seem to know what to do? Sometimes students ask a teacher whom they respect for her or his opinion. Your guidance counselor is professionally trained to help you make decisions about academic options, such as where to apply for college, and find resources for personal problems like where to go for help for a drug or alcohol problem. Trust your gut feeling about people; if they seem trustworthy and wise, you might ask for their input or draw upon their expertise.

Books and Libraries

If you need factual or background information before making a decision, your school or public library can help. Suppose you are considering a career field like computer programming. Your library probably has books on this subject that are specifically focused on career exploration. The librarian could work with you to find the resources you need.

Authorities on a Given Subject

Suppose you are about to buy your first car. You can't afford a new one, and you don't want to throw away the money you've saved on a lemon. Here it would be important to consult with someone who knows cars well, like a mechanic, before deciding whether or not to buy a certain car. Professionals who offer their advice may charge for their services, but the investment is usually worth it.

Counselors and Clergy

Social workers, therapists, guidance counselors, psychologists, ministers, rabbis, and priests have all been professionally trained to listen well. They can help you ask the right questions of yourself as you work toward finding answers.

People whom you trust can help you reach your own good decisions.

You might talk to a neighbor or an old friend for advice on
a decision you must make.

Sometimes it helps to write down your feelings about a decision you need to make.

Chapter 4

Listening to Yourself

Voices Inside You

Even before you ask someone else for advice, you are getting the opinions of other people. You (and everyone else) carry around voices inside you from memories of what you have been taught when you were young. These thoughts influence how you feel about yourself and, as a result, how you act. For example, you may have been told to "Act like a lady," meaning that you should be sweet and accepting, or to "Act like a man," meaning that you should be tough and unemotional, no matter how you are feeling. Perhaps you were instructed, "If you can't say anything nice, don't say anything at all," or "Only sissies cry." These voices tell you what you "should" do, on the basis of someone else's notion of proper behavior. When you recognize how these thoughts and memories influence you,

you can think more clearly when making a decision.

Being Your Own Friend

When you hear these voices in your mind, try to notice if they are helpful or hurtful. Are they voices that encourage you and place things in perspective, or are they ready to put you down and beat you up for a simple mistake? Respond to the voices that are on your side.

Chris is deciding if he should go to the prom or not. On one hand, he thinks that it might be fun, and some of his friends are going. On the other hand, it is an expensive night, he's not sure whom he would ask to go with him, and a few of the guys he hangs out with are putting down the whole idea of going to this big dance. He finds himself thinking about this a lot as the dance gets closer, and he says to himself:

"I'd probably have a lousy time, because not all my friends will be there. Who would want to go with me anyway? I probably couldn't get a date. It's such a hassle renting a tuxedo and figuring out all the arrangements. What a waste of money. Besides, I'm not a good dancer; people might make fun of me."

Chris is being his own enemy here; the voices inside him are not giving him a chance to try something he might enjoy. But when Ann, a girl Chris likes, asks him to the prom, he realizes that he does want to go. The voices inside him begin to sound different.

"The prom is a once-in-a-lifetime experience, and it should be fun. Sure it costs money, but I've saved up enough to pay for my ticket, and Ann will pay for hers. I know enough people who will be there—we'll all sit together and have a good time. I can dance well enough; besides, you don't have to dance all night."

Here Chris is sounding like a friend to himself, since this voice is encouraging and supportive. Now he feels happy and eager when he thinks about going to the prom. The voices inside his head change, and his emotions also tell him that this decision is right.

Listening to Your Feelings

When you take the time to listen to yourself, your own emotions are a big help in figuring out whether a decision is right or not. Do you feel excited and energized by one option? Does another make you sigh with resignation? Does one possibility make you worried or nervous about what could happen as a result? Does a certain decision suddenly make you feel at ease? Listen to those feelings.

Matthew is new in his school and eager to make friends. So when Bob invites him to go to a party on Saturday night, Matthew looks forward to it. But when Saturday night comes and they walk into the party, Matthew starts to feel uneasy. He knows right away that the parents of the house are not at home. The living room reeks of pot. The lights are very low, the music is blaring, and everyone seems to be huddled in groups of two or three in corners of the room. Matthew notices a number of people popping pills. His first instinct is to call his parents to pick him up, but he doesn't want to seem like a baby, so he acts as if nothing is wrong. Then Bob comes over to him.

"Hey Matthew, my man."

Matthew can tell that Bob is already high on something.

"I've got a Welcome to the Neighborhood present for you," Bob says, holding out a little blue pill. "Enjoy, pal," he continues, and slaps him on the back.

Matthew's stomach knots up. He feels scared and confused, and he knows that he does not want to ingest this mystery pill.

"Um . . . thanks," he says, taking the pill from Bob's hand. "Could you excuse me a minute?"

Matthew goes to the bathroom and throws the pill down the sink; then he makes some loud vomiting noises. When he comes out, Bob is looking bewildered.

"Sorry, man, but I feel ill—it's all the smoke—I'm allergic," Matthew lies. "I've got to go."

Matthew finds a phone and calls his parents, then waits outside for them. He feels relieved to be away from this drug scene.

Matthew was uncomfortable. His feelings told him that this was a dangerous place that could cause him to mess up his body and his mind. Instead of going along with what the people around him were doing, Matthew decided to leave a potentially harmful situation. He listened to his own emotions.

Matthew also listened to his conscience. Matthew's parents and teachers had taught him that taking drugs is scary and stupid. An inner voice clearly told Matthew that this was the wrong thing to do.

Listening to Your Body

Your body also gives you clues about what is right for you. Just as Matthew felt a knot in the pit of his stomach when he was offered drugs, physical reactions like sweaty palms, tense muscles, a dry mouth, rapid heartbeat, or perspiration are your body's way of telling you something. Maybe a decision is causing you joyful excitement and so your heart is pounding, or maybe you feel dread and your legs turn to jelly.

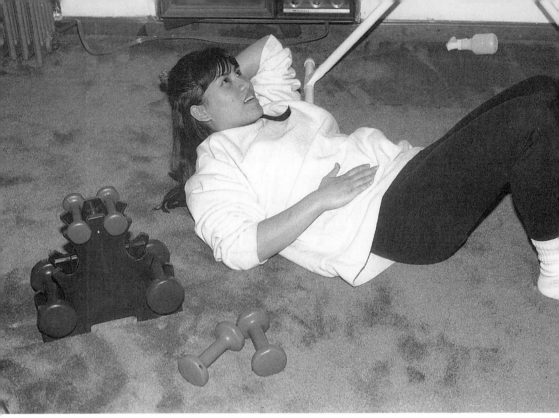

Exercise is one way you might choose to deal with your body's reaction to a decision in your life.

Either way, your body is letting you know that this decision is powerful.

What Do You Want?

You are the best expert on yourself, and you know how a certain choice will or won't work for you. Some people listen to themselves by writing in a journal or diary. Others go on walks or jogs so they can sort out possibilities in their mind. When making a decision, remember that your own opinion is the most important.

Chapter 5

Steps to Making Good Decisions

Whithen you need to make a big decision, do you agonize over the possibilities in your mind? This may leave you feeling more confused. However, if you had to figure out a math problem, you would probably take out pencil and paper and follow the steps needed to solve it. Sometimes making a decision is also easier when you have a process to follow. Here are some steps that might help you address situations head-on.

1. Ask yourself, "What's my main goal?"

Allison can't decide if she should get a job after school. Her friend Jennifer works in a clothing store where there is an open position that Allison could probably get. Allison feels torn. She earns some money baby-sitting but thinks it would be great to have extra income for clothes and going out with her friends. But if she has to be at the store a few afternoons a week, she won't be able to try out for a lead in the school play. She is unsure what to do until she asks herself, "What do I want for myself in the long run?" Then she realizes that what is most important to her is getting into a good college. Being involved in extracurricular activities and having more time to study would help her college applications more than working at a store. Allison decides to not to apply for the job, even though it would have been fun to have the money.

By asking herself, "What do I want to achieve?" Allison has made a decision that helps her accomplish her goals by thinking about what really matters to her. Sometimes simply looking at where you want to go leads you to decisions that take you there.

2. Explore all the options

Tony's friends are planning to go to the movies together on Sunday afternoon. Tony would like to go, but he's not sure if he can afford it. Ever since his parents got divorced money has been tight, and Tony uses the money he earns from odd jobs to pay for his own clothes. He feels too embarrassed to admit this to his friends and decides to make up an excuse and just stay home. His mother notices that

Budgeting your money involves determining your priorities before deciding how and where to spend your money.

he seems a bit glum and asks him what is the matter. When Tony tells her, his mother suggests that he and his friends might find something else to do. She suggests that they play football or come over to the house to watch a game on television. It would be a cheaper afternoon, and they could still have a good time together.

Sometimes there are solutions that might not be obvious at first. If you can't figure out what to do, complete this sentence: "In the best of all possible worlds . . .". Tony thought that he could either go out with his friends or stay home by himself. But ideally, Tony can find a way to have a good time with his friends without spending a lot. They might play a game or catch some sports on television. If his friends still wanted to go out, Tony might meet up with them after the movie. He could budget a certain amount of money for his time with them and be careful not to spend any more. He might also decide not to buy any more new clothes for a while and use the money from his jobs for going out with friends in the future. Often there are more options than the ones presented; you just need to be creative and find them.

3. Gather information and other helpful input

Kathryn is in shock. Her period was three weeks late, and so she bought a home pregnancy test. Her fears were realized when she discovered that she was pregnant. She and her boyfriend Darroll had been sleeping together for six months. They always used a condom, but one time it broke. Kathryn can't believe her bad luck and doesn't know what to do. But she knows that she needs to decide soon.

She tells Darroll that she is pregnant, and he swears that he'll stand by her no matter what happens. He says he'll even marry her if she wants. But Kathryn does not want to get married at age seventeen. She looks in the phone book and calls her

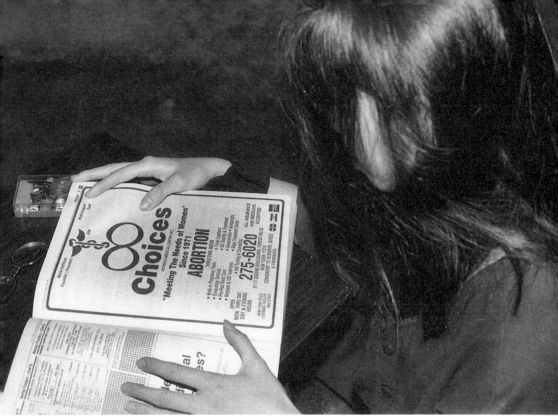

In order to make the decision that is right for you, you must weigh your options carefully, and consider all the possible consequences of your final choice.

local Planned Parenthood center, which arranges for her to meet with a counselor. Next Kathryn goes to the library and reads about teen pregnancy. In a book she discovers an organization in Washington, D.C., called the National Committee for Adoption. She gets their number from directory assistance and calls them; they then send her information on adoption alternatives. After reading the literature they sent, she doesn't feel that she could give up the baby once it was born.

Kathryn had never thought of herself as very religious, but now she is praying a lot. After a few days of soul-searching, she decides to tell her mother what has happened. At first her mother is mad, but then she feels upset and worried about Kathryn's future. Kathryn is too. She knows one acquaintance from school who dropped out the year before to have a baby and is now living on welfare. Kathryn knows that abortion is safe and legal, and she does not feel that the embryo inside her is a life yet. She decides to end her pregnancy.

Kathryn uses information and others' opinions to help her reach this difficult decision. Darroll says he will stay by her if she has the baby, and her mother is concerned about what having a baby would do to Kathryn. She reads about teen pregnancy in books and goes over the information from Planned Parenthood and the National Committee for Adoption. She thinks long and hard about what to do, and knows that ultimately the decision is hers. Kathryn does not believe that having an abortion is morally wrong, and so she chooses this option in good conscience.

4. List the arguments for and against (pro and con) a certain choice

Before she goes through with the abortion, Kathryn starts having doubts. She wonders what the operation will be like and stays awake one night worrying about this. Since she can't sleep and feels tormented, Kathryn turns on the light, goes to her desk, and takes out pencil and paper. She makes two columns to write down her thoughts so she can think more clearly about this important decision.

HAVING A BABY

Pro	**Con**
• *bring life into this world*	• *not ready to be a mother now*
• *babies are fun and cute*	• *babies require a lot of work*
• *have baby and give it up for adoption*	• *unsure if I could give up baby*
• *have baby and marry Darroll (?)*	• *too young to get married*
	• *going to high school while pregnant, worse dropping out*
	• *pain of giving birth*
	• *no job skills to support self and baby*
	• *going to college is very difficult*
	• *having a good career is very difficult*

Once Kathryn has written down her reasons, she feels comforted. Seeing the list in front of her helps her to understand what caused her to make this choice. She knows that this is the right decision for her at this time.

5. Ask yourself if this decision hurts you or someone else

Jed is nervous because he has to take the Scholastic Aptitude Test (SAT) for college entry in five days. He has studied for weeks, but he has a problem freezing up on tests. He is sitting in the cafeteria during lunch talking about the test with some friends when a guy he knows, Michael, pipes up.

"Jed, no need to be so nervous," Michael begins.

"That's easy for you to say, but I have a hard time taking tests . . ." Jed explains.

"Listen," Michael continues, "I'll lend you my friend." With a wink, Michael reaches into his backpack and pulls out a small pocket dictionary. "Just use this for the verbal section. The gym where you take the test is so huge, and all those proctors do is sit at their desks anyway. I'm sure that this paper pal brought my score up 100 points."

Since his friends are looking at him, Jed takes the dictionary.

"Uh . . . thanks, Michael," Jed says.

But as the day of the test draws near, Jed isn't sure what to do. Would it be right to use a dictionary when this is clearly cheating? On the other hand, Jed feels that if no one finds out, what harm is done? Besides, no one is really hurt by it, and the difference just might help him get into his top choice of schools.

Jed needs to decide if using a dictionary is the right (moral) or wrong (immoral) action to take. Since he finds himself rationalizing, he is probably on the wrong track. While it may not be obvious, cheating on the exam does hurt people. First, Jed hurts himself. If he already gets nervous on tests, the added stress of worrying about being caught with a dictionary could cause him to think less clearly. Cheating would also be unfair to the other students who studied for the exam and took it honestly. A decision that hurts you or others is wrong and should be avoided.

6. Think through the consequences or results of your decision

As Jed is debating about what to do, he pictures what might happen if he used the dictionary during the test. First he envisions himself going into the exam room very calm and collected. He imagines taking the test, sneaking peeks at the dictionary, then later getting a great score. When he sees how well he did, Jed figures that he'll be so happy about it he'll just forget about the cheating and not feel bad at all. That's one possible scenario.

On the other hand, Jed thinks about the possible negative consequences of cheating. He imagines getting a good test score but feeling miserable about knowing that it really doesn't belong to him. Worse, he wonders about getting caught. Suppose the proctor sees him cheating and takes the dictionary from him in front of everyone. He would be forced to leave the test and would be reported to school officials. This would seriously hurt his chances of getting into a good college. On top of all that, Jed knows that the word would travel around the school about what had happened. He thinks about how horribly embarrassed he would feel in front of his friends and teachers.

Before making a decision, you need to think through what might happen as a result. Ask yourself how you might benefit or lose from different outcomes. Also consider how your decision would affect anyone else involved in the situation. Once you weigh the consequences, the right decision may be more obvious.

7. Take time to make your decision

As the test date approaches, Jed is still undecided. Michael keeps on telling him what a breeze the exam will be with the dictionary. So Jed decides to "try on" each decision for a day to see how they feel. On the Thursday before the test he thinks that he will take the dictionary in with him. He notices that he feels worried and his stomach knots up. He feels uncomfortable talking with friends about the exam, as if he already had something to hide. On Friday, he thinks that he will not *take the dictionary in with him. This time, Jed is a little more relaxed. He doesn't worry about getting caught cheating; he just thinks about getting in the room and giving the exam his best shot. He decides that this decision feels better, and so he follows his own instinct and takes the test honestly.*

Here Jed has some time to make his decision, and he uses it well. There are times, however, when you need to decide something immediately. If you need to make a decision right away (such as what to put on for school that day), you might whiz the possibilities through your mind quickly. At times, though, someone might pressure you to make a decision before you need to or are ready. If someone keeps pressuring you, it is best either to let him know when you will give him an answer or just to refuse.

8. Make your decision

By following this process, you will have a way to address decisions you need to make. You can develop positive thinking habits, just as you might have good habits for taking care of your appearance or improving your mind. When you take solid steps to make your decisions, you can proceed with confidence.

Chapter 6

Making Mistakes

Whenever you make a decision, you run the risk of making a mistake. Perhaps you decide something that gets you in trouble. Maybe you end up feeling embarrassed or ashamed. A bad decision is one that hurts you or someone else. When you need to choose between possibilities, it is good to ask yourself if the result could be harmful to anyone. If so, that decision should be avoided.

But sometimes you might make a decision with good intentions, only to discover that things didn't work out the way you planned. You regret what you have done and feel miserable. When that happens, it is best to confront the mistake head-on. By dealing with the problem honestly, you avoid further complications later. Also, admitting that you have done something wrong usually earns respect. You feel better about your own ability, instead of feeling guilty or full of self-pity. Ask yourself, "What can I do to make the best of this situation?" When you try to learn from what has happened, even making a poor decision can help you in the future.

How Much Does This Matter?

When a decision you make does not turn out well, first ask yourself, "How much does this matter?" Without perspective, you might stay mad at yourself for a mistake that is not very serious. Don't blow a small issue way out of proportion. If the problem is small, just fix it and go on. Recognizing that a problem exists can help you correct it so that the situation doesn't become worse.

Carolina and her friends have decided to hang out together and rent a movie for the night. Since everyone is coming over to Carolina's house, she went to get the movie.

That night Elizabeth, Rosa, and Marisol gather at Carolina's house. The popcorn is popped, the soda is poured, and they are all looking forward to a fun film. But the movie stinks. After just a few minutes, they start to get bored. Carolina sees that her friends aren't having a good time, and she feels lousy because she selected this movie. Elizabeth murmurs, "Great movie, Carolina. NOT." Carolina hears this but pretends she doesn't. "Oh great, I should have

You may fear displeasing someone such as a boyfriend or girlfriend with a decision you make. This fear is common, but try not to let it stop you from deciding what's best for you.

gotten something else," she thinks. Carolina continues to feel awful. She starts listing in her mind all the other movies that the video store had that would have been better. She gets mad at herself for ruining what should have been a good time. Over and over she tells herself that no one is having fun. Without anyone's realizing it, Carolina makes sure that she feels the worst of anyone.

Then she stops herself. "This isn't such a big deal," she remembers. She walks over to the VCR and puts it on pause. "Okay, you guys," she announces, standing in front of the TV, "anyone care to see the end of this? . . . Do you want to go get another movie? It's not too late. Or do you want to just hang out and forget about watching a movie altogether?"

Then Elizabeth pipes up, "What's on TV?"

"Take a look," Carolina says, handing her the weekly television schedule.

"I'm tired of watching anyway," adds Rosa. "Why don't we just play Pictionary?"

"Yeah, that's a good idea," Marisol chimes in. "Carolina and I will team up against you two. How about it?"

Within minutes the girls are laughing at their silly drawings and having a great time. Recognizing that she had made a decision that disappointed everyone and then doing something about it, Carolina was able to do what she set out to do: have a fun night with her friends.

You may not realize until much later that a decision you have made, such as drinking alcohol with friends, was wrong. It is best to admit the mistake and learn from it.

Bigger Mistakes

Some mistakes that you make are more serious because the consequences that result from what you said or did can be very harmful. Because you run the risk of getting in big trouble, you probably hope that you don't get caught and later may want to pretend that the situation did not happen at all. It is also very tempting to try to shift the blame onto someone else. However, bigger mistakes usually lead to deeper investigation. If you have made a mistake, you are more honest with
yourself and others if you own up to what you've

done, correct it in any way you can, and make sure that you don't do it again.

"Hey, Kev, thanks for a great time," Louis calls to his buddy, Kevin, as he leaves the party.

"You, homeboy, are a party animal," Kevin jokes, putting his arm around Lou's shoulder. "You really did your fair share in knocking off those kegs of beer. You need some help getting home?"

"Me? Nah, I feel great, never felt better, yup, I am a-okay," Louis shouts over the music. He weaves his way to his parents' car, looking unsteady on his feet. When he gets behind the wheel he vaguely recalls being told not to drink and drive.

"That doesn't apply to me," Louis thinks.

On his way home. Louis doesn't notice a red light. Another car screeches to a halt and just barely misses him. The driver pulls over and screams at Louis. Louis tells himself what an idiot the other driver is and keeps on going. When he gets home. Louis tries to pull his car into the driveway, but he misses. Instead he drives into the "SLOW—Children at Play" sign in front of his house. The front bumper gets banged in and the sign doubles over on itself. Louis starts to realize that he has been driving drunk. He feels awful about the car and relieved that his parents did not wake up at the sound of the crash. In the morning he will have to decide what to tell them, but for now all he wants to do is sleep.

When Louis wakes up, his parents are downstairs

*having breakfast. He wonders what he should tell
them. On one hand, he could make up a lie that the
neighbor's cat ran in front of the car while he was
pulling into the driveway, so he swerved to avoid
hitting it and crashed into the sign. Or he could tell
them the truth. Not admitting that he drove drunk
feels easier, but Louis also knows that it may catch
up with him. His lie doesn't make much sense
because if he had seen the cat he could have just
stopped the car, so his parents may not believe him.
Also, Louis wonders if that other driver took down
his license plate number and will report him. Louis
decides that it is better to come clean now than have
to keep worrying about what might happen if his
parents found out later. He will tell them what he
did wrong and let them know how sorry he is.
Maybe he should to offer to pay for the damage to
the car, even though he knows that won't be cheap.
Louis knows that a car with a drunk driver becomes
a death machine, and he decides never to repeat
such a stupid mistake. With this resolved, he goes
downstairs to face his parents.*

By admitting that he has made this mistake,
Louis is showing maturity that should gain him
some respect. Of course, his parents won't be
happy when they learn what he has done, but they
may appreciate his honesty. Louis may have to
suffer some consequences, like not being able to
drive his parents' car for a while, but at least he

doesn't have to keep carrying this around on his conscience. By admitting his mistake, making amends for it, and promising not to repeat it, Louis has the chance to start again.

When you face your mistakes head-on, you keep problems from getting bigger. It may take a lot of strength and conviction to change a situation, but often you will gain the respect of others—and yourself. Difficult decisions can become learning situations. Remember that everyone makes mistakes—it's what you do afterward that can set you apart.

Chapter 7

Deciding to Succeed

Everyone wants to succeed. Ask a teenager, "What do you want to do with your life?" and no one is going to say, "Become a prisoner." You probably have your own dreams of what you would like to do; making good decisions will help you achieve your goals.

But not everyone starts with the same opportunities. Many teenagers today have to cope with the stress of family divorce, financial troubles, drug and alcohol addiction, violence in school, young pregnancy, and other difficult issues. Images in the media and on television show families that work everything out in half an hour. Because real issues are not resolved so easily, you may end up feeling trapped.

James is concerned that he might be gay. His whole life he has been attracted to men, but he keeps this inside. His friends make nasty jokes about gay

*characters on TV and famous people who have come
out as homosexuals. James says nothing. Now his
parents have started trying to get him to date their
friends' daughter, but James always makes excuses.*

*James wishes that he had someone to talk to about
these feelings, but he is afraid that people will be
mean and make fun of him. But if he really starts to
look, he can find supportive places where he can ask
questions. He might go to his library and look for
books and articles on teenage sexuality. He might
look in the phone book for a teen hotline and see if
he could find a referral to an agency that helps teenagers talk about sexual orientation. James might talk
with an adult whom he trusts just so that he wouldn't
have to keep all his feelings inside. These steps might
help James sort through his mixed emotions.*

If your options seem limited, think hard about
what choices there may be. Look for possibilities,
create new ones if you have to, and decide what is
best for you. If you get discouraged by some
people, find others who will encourage you. Listen
to yourself and what feels honest.

Sometimes it may seem as if you have too many
good choices. You may be overwhelmed by all the
options that appeal to you. This can leave you
feeling lost and confused.

*Tamecka was accepted into her three top choices
of colleges, and she is having a hard time deciding*

where to go. Hollister College is a small liberal-arts school, the State University at Springfield is large and public, and the Woudenberg University is private and prestigious. All have strong departments in business and economics, which is what she plans to study. The state university is less expensive, but the other two have offered her good scholarships. After visiting the schools and writing lists of pros and cons for each institution, and talking to professors and students, Tamecka decides to go with her gut feeling. She chooses the state university, because here the African-American community is strongest. Tamecka thinks it would be the best place for her to thrive.

Making thoughtful, intelligent decisions helps you to thrive. As you grow older, you will have more and more opportunities to decide for yourself. Each gives you the chance to help yourself, while being fair to whoever else is involved. When you make up your own mind, instead of going along with others against your own better judgment, you are becoming a stronger person. Even your mistakes will benefit you when you correct them and learn from the experience.

When you think through the possibilities and trust yourself, you will be helping yourself in everyday and extraordinary situations. One of the best ways to succeed is by learning—and deciding—to decide well.

Glossary—*Explaining New Words*

accomplish   To achieve or make happen.

advice   Opinion, guidance.

aggressive   Forceful, pursuing what one wants with little regard for anything or anyone else.

assertive   Positive, confident, self-assured, respectful.

conscience   Inner awareness or voice telling you that something is right or wrong.

consequence   Result; the effect of an action.

conviction   Stick-to-it-iveness, determination.

dominate   To control one or more individuals or a situation.

immoral   With highly unfair, selfish, or evil intention or purpose.

manipulate   To control or manage with hidden motives.

moral   Honest, upright character or behavior.

opinion   One's own thoughts, advice, or point of view.

passive   Not speaking up or taking action.

passive-aggressive   Going after objectives by lack of words or action: manipulating by silence or inactivity.

peer pressure   Influence from people your own age to be like them.

perspective   Judgment of a person or situation from a certain point of view; an overall view.

rationalize   To explain with false or exaggerated reasons in order to convince someone else or yourself.

Where to Go For Help

In the United States

Alcoholics Anonymous
  (AA)
P.O. Box 459
Grand Central Station
New York, NY 10163

STOPP (Students to
  Offset Peer Pressure)
P.O. Box 103, Department S
Hudson, NH 03051-0103

SADD (Students Against
  Drunk Driving)
Box 800
Marlboro, MA 01750
(508) 481-3568

"Just Say No" International
2101 Webster Street
Oakland Creek, CA 94612
(510) 451-6666

TARGET—Helping
  Students Cope with
  Tobacco, Alcohol, and
  Other Drugs
11724 NW Plaza Circle
P.O. Box 20626
Kansas City, MO 64195
(816) 464-5400

Help, Inc.
638 South Street
Philadelphia, PA 19147
(215) 546-7766

In Canada

Alcohol and Drug
  Dependency
  Information and
  Counseling Services
  (ADDICS)
#2, 2471 1/2 Portage
  Avenue
Winnipeg, MB R3J 0N6
(204) 831-1999

Narcotics Anonymous
P.O. Box 7500
Station A
Toronto, ON M5W 1P9
(416) 691-9519

Alcoholics Anonymous
#502, Intergroup Office
234 Enlington Avenue E.
Toronto, ON M4P 1K5
(416) 487-5591

For Further Reading

Arnold, John D. *The Complete Problem Solver.* New York: Wiley, 1992.

———. *Make Up Your Mind!* New York: Amacom, 1978.

Feller, Robyn M. *Everything You Need to Know About Peer Pressure.* New York: Rosen, 1993.

McFarland, Rhoda. *Coping Through Assertiveness.* New York: Rosen, 1992.

Newman, Mildred, and Berkowitz, Bernard. *Take Charge of Your Life.* New York: Harcourt, Brace, Jovanovich, 1977.

Sinetar, Marsha. *Self-Esteem Is Just an Idea We Have About Ourselves: La Autoestima No Es Mas Que Una Idea Que Tenemos Acerca De Nosotros Mismos.* New York: Paulist Press, 1990, bilingual.

Smith, Sandra Lee. *Coping with Decision-Making.* New York: Rosen, 1993.

Index

About the Author
Julie Parker is an ordained minister in the United
Methodist Church with professional experience in
counseling. She has written numerous books and articles
for teenagers.

Photo Credits
Cover by Michael Brandt; p. 6 by Katherine Hsu; p. 50 by
Maria Moreno; all other photos by Kim Sonsky.